the little book of

MISCHIEF

the little book of MISCHIEF

Raymond Glynne

ARCTURUS

PICTURE CREDITS – AP Photos: 33 (David Longstreath). **AP/Press Association Images:** 8, 42, 69. **Ardea:** 6 (John Daniels), 9 (Uno Berggren), 12 (John Daniels), 15 (M. Watson), 16 (John Daniels), 17 (John Daniels), 19 (John Daniels), 20 (Jean Michel Labat), 21 (Chris Knights), 30 (John Daniels), 31 (Maurice Walker), 32 (Jean Michel Labat), 35 (Jean Michel Labat), 36 (John Cancalosi), 37 (John Daniels), 41 (Brian Bevan), 43 (Jean Michel Labat), 44 (Roy Glen), 47 (Jean Michel Labat), 48 (Jean Michel Labat), 49 (Jean Michel Labat), 50 (Pat Morris), 51 (Jean Michel Labat), 53 (Yann Arthus-Bertrand), 54 (Jean Michel Labat), 55 (Brian Bevan), 57 (Duncan Usher), 58 (Rolf Kopfle), 63 (Chris Harvey), 67 (Brian Bevan), 73 (Brian Bevan), 74 (Brian Bevan), 75 (John Daniels), 76 (John Daniels), 77 (Jean Michel Labat), 78 (M. Watson), 79 (John Daniels), 80 (John Daniels), 82 (Duncan Usher), 86 (Johan de Meester), 91 (John Daniels), 92 (Tom & Pat Leeson). **Corbis:** 11, 13 (Moshe Shai), 14 (Keren Su), 22 (Dureuil Philippe/És), 23 (Frank May/dpa), 24 (DLILLC), 25 (DLILLC), 26 (Chris Collins), 27 (Renee Lynn), 28 (Ocean), 29 (Wolfgang Kumm/dpa), 38 (Halden Krog/epa), 39 (Steve Kazlowski/Science Faction), 45 (Steve Kazlowski/Science Faction), 46 (Radius Images), 56 (Herbert Kehrer), 59 (David Aubrey), 60 (DLILLC), 61 (Keren Su), 65 (Nigel Pavitt/JAI), 66 (Daniel J. Cox), 71 (Michael DeYoung), 72 (Tom Stewart), 87 (Frans Lanting), 88 (Gopal Chitrakar/Reuters), 89 (Kevin Schafer), 90 (Thomas Kitchin & Victoria Hurst/First Light), 93 (Frans Lanting), 94 (Frank Lukasseck), 95 (Wayne Hutchinson/AgStock Images), 96 (Don Mason). **DJSPhotography:** 70. **EMPICS:** 40 (Jeff Moore). **Mircea Costina:** 52. **PhotoAlto:** 85. **Press Association Images:** 34, 62, 68, 81, 83. **Shutterstock:** cover, 7, 10, 18, 64, 84

ARCTURUS

This edition published in 2012 by Arcturus Publishing Limited
26/27 Bickels Yard, 151–153 Bermondsey Street,
London SE1 3HA

ISBN: 978-1-84858-184-5
AD001966EN

Printed in China

Mischief: we know it's wrong, but we can't help loving it. Why is that? Why can't we decide one way or the other? Why do parents find themselves wanting to laugh while they scold their children? Why do we smile when we see mischief perpetrated against others? And why does the mere thought of mischief make us all feel a little bit naughty?

Isn't it time we all agreed that mischief is marvellous? Unless, of course, it happens to be your trousers that are flying at the top of the flagpole.

When it comes to making mischief, two heads are
better than one.

It's always good to have an appreciative audience.

And you need a bit of brawn to complement your mischievous brain.

Go into business with a lookalike and you'll keep
everyone guessing.

Then again, some partnerships you'd never suspect.

It's hard not to be mischievous when there's so much temptation around.

I mean, how is anyone supposed to resist this!

Try to look the other way. Go on, just keep walking.

Oh dear! This is going to end badly.

OK, let's just leave it there, shall we?

Some say showing off is a sign of insecurity.

But if you've got it, flaunt it!

A silly hat always gets a chuckle.

But try to keep a straight face.

And if all else fails, do your funny dance.

There's mischief, and there's plain bad manners.

Didn't anyone tell you not to pull faces?

Now that's just asking for trouble!

You think you're safe behind that fence?

Oh now really! Where were you brought up?

Ta-dah! Instant makeover.

What's the point of puddles if you can't jump in them?

It's a little too late for 'sorry'.

Who is responsible for this mess?

I want that table so clean you can see your face in it.

Why does other people's food always taste better?

Mmm, forbidden fruit!

Oops! I seem to have drunk the lot.

It's all in the presentation, you know.

Who can blame you for the occasional indulgence?

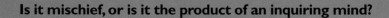

Is it mischief, or is it the product of an inquiring mind?

A creative streak should be allowed to flourish.

Everyone needs a hobby.

Work out in advance who's the driver and who's the mechanic.

A little time spent reading the manual will pay dividends.

Some things are worth the risk.

What's the worst that can happen?

We all need a little exhilaration in our lives.

Even if you're not entirely confident.

Just hold on tight and enjoy the ride.

Who put this here? Very considerate of them...

Bird table, you say?

Look! All clean!

If I can just… reach… another… inch.

Ha ha! They'll never find me in here.

There's nothing more satisfying than an unsuspecting victim.

Oh, this is going to be good!

Just a little nip and… Gotcha!

That's it, just keep walking.

Oh my! There goes another terrified paper boy.

Don't you love it when a plan comes together?

Laugh? I nearly fell out of my wheel!

There's nothing wrong with a little harmless fun.

Laugh and the whole world laughs with you…

...Well, with the odd exception.

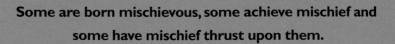

Some are born mischievous, some achieve mischief and
some have mischief thrust upon them.

Why hog all the mischief to yourself when you can share it with a friend?

But be careful about the company you keep.

Some people's idea of mischief might be very different from yours.

Remember your individuality and don't bow to peer pressure.

Do you think they wanted that bin?

Now that wasn't supposed to happen, was it?

Ah, pulled the wrong way. Sorry!

Well, you can still see through them.

If all else fails, smile!

Mischief makers always get caught in the end.

It becomes an addiction that they have to feed.

They lose patience and get caught in the act.

They get overconfident and careless.

Or they get cocky and can't help showing off their prize.

The art of keeping a straight face can help you get away with anything.

A little sweet innocence goes a long way.

Yeah, but not too serious. That just looks suspicious.

Act casually and you might just pull it off.

That's it. And if you can whistle too…

If you're going to hide, you'll have to do better than that!

Just because you can't see us, doesn't mean we can't see you.

Oh, for goodness' sake!

That's a bit more like it. But try to resist the urge to peek.

Good lord! A rock with ears!

First rule of mischief: know when to run away!

Or tiptoe quietly, whichever you think is best.

Make sure you can remember the way out.

Try not to draw attention to yourself.

And don't get stuck!

Beware of mischief backfiring on you.

There's nothing more humiliating than having to wait for help.

Try not to overstretch yourself.

Don't all make the same mistake at once.

Or you could end up the butt of your own joke.